BREATHE, THINK, DO

WITH

ELMO

Problem Solving for
LITTLE MONSTERS

by Sesame Workshop and Robin Newman
Illustrated by Ernie Kwiat

Parents and caregivers, turn to page 46 for a resource guide!

RP|KIDS
PHILADELPHIA

Running Press Kids
Hachette Book Group
1290 Avenue of the Americas, New York, NY 10104
www.runningpress.com/rpkids
@RP_Kids

Printed in China

First Edition: July 2021

Published by Running Press Kids, an imprint of Perseus Books, LLC, a subsidiary of Hachette Book Group, Inc. The Running Press Kids name and logo is a trademark of the Hachette Book Group.

The Hachette Speakers Bureau provides a wide range of authors for speaking events. To find out more, go to www.hachettespeakersbureau.com or call (866) 376-6591.

The publisher is not responsible for websites (or their content) that are not owned by the publisher.

Print book cover and interior design by Frances J. Soo Ping Chow.
Illustrated by Ernie Kwiat

Library of Congress Control Number: 2019957400

ISBN: 978-0-7624-7038-9

1010

10 9 8 7 6 5 4 3 2 1

Hello, reader! It is your old pal Grover. Thank you so much for opening my little book. I have been waiting and *waiting* for someone to open this book. And you did it! It is very hard to wait, even for a cute and adorable monster like myself. When I am having one of those days, I remember three important things:

BREATHE,
THINK,
DO!

First, I **BREATHE**.

I take three slow, deep breaths, breathing in through my nose and out through my mouth.

Try it with me!

ONE.
TWO.
THREE.

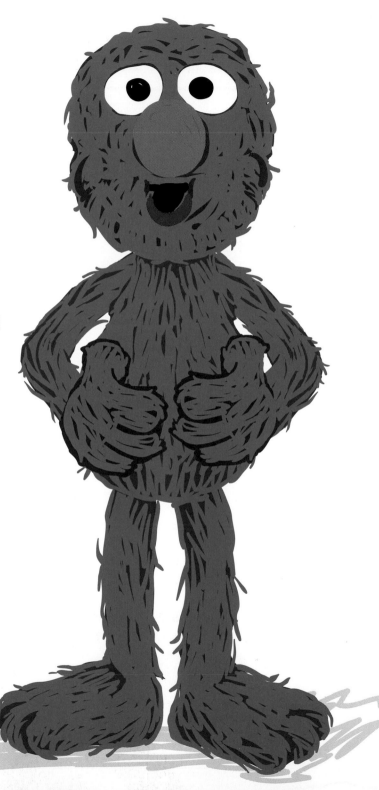

Then, I **THINK** of three things I can do to solve my problem. For example, when I need help with waiting for someone to open this book, I can . . .

1. Sing a song.

2. Draw some pictures.

3. Visit a friend.

And then, I **DO**! I choose one way and see how it goes. If it doesn't work, I can try something else.

Today, Elmo needs our help solving some problems! Let's think of three ways he can solve them, then turn the page for the solutions! Are you ready? Get set! Let's try them all!

Elmo was so excited! He was going to ride the big-kid roller coaster with Baby David.

MONSTER COASTER

6

But there was a problem.

"I'm sorry, but you must be this tall to ride on the roller coaster."

Elmo stood on his tippy, tippy, tippy toes.

But the operator shook his head no. "I'm sorry, friend. You are not tall enough for this ride."

Then Bert and Ernie walked past him onto the ride. "Hi, Elmo!" they said. Even though they were his friends, Elmo didn't say hi back. He just wanted to stomp away. Elmo was feeling **JEALOUS**.

 "Psst! Elmo needs your help. Let's **BREATHE** together! Put your hands on your tummy and take three slow, deep breaths in through your nose and out through your mouth."

Let's **THINK** of three ways to help Elmo feel better.

1. Elmo and his mommy can go on a
ride that is just right for him.
Turn to page 10!

2. Elmo can play a game instead.
Turn to page 12!

3. Elmo and his mommy can walk around
the park and get a special treat.
Turn to page 14!

Now, let's **DO**! Turn to solution, **1**, **2**, or **3**.

INFORMATION

🎠 MERRY-GO-ROUND

🏺 CHUGGA-CHOO-CHOO

🐹 WHACK-A-MOLE

"Mommy, can you help Elmo find a ride for little monsters?"
"I sure can. Want to try the merry-go-round? Or how about
the Chugga-Choo-Choo train?"

"Elmo wants to ride both!"

Elmo ran to the whack-a-mole game hoping he might win a gigantic stuffed fish for Baby David.

"You must hit three moles to win the gigantic fish," said the game operator.

One. *Hit!* Two. *Hit!* Three. Uh-oh! *Miss!*

"Sorry! You didn't win the gigantic fish, but you did win a little stuffed fish."

"Hooray! Baby David can have a fish friend."

"Let's see what else is at the park!" says Elmo's mommy.

"Yes! Elmo and Mommy will walk around and look at everything. And then can we get a special treat?"

14

15

Elmo was going to play his first game of T-ball today.

"Elmo has never played T-ball. Have Zoe and Abby?"

"Yes! I like running the bases!" said Zoe.

"Me too!" said Abby. "I also love catching the ball way up in the air!"

"Welcome," said Coach. "I'd like everyone to take turns hitting the ball off the tee."

First, Zoe swung the bat. A hit! Abby was up next, and then it was Elmo's turn. But he wasn't ready!

"No! Elmo can't! Elmo doesn't know how!"

Elmo was shaking. His heart was beating fast. He wasn't sure if he could hit the ball! He was feeling **NERVOUS**.

 "Psst! Elmo needs your help. Let's **BREATHE** together! Put your hands on your tummy and take three slow, deep breaths in through your nose and out through your mouth."

Let's **THINK** of three ways to help Elmo feel better.

1. Elmo can watch, learn, and talk to himself about what he needs to do.
Turn to page 20!

2. Elmo can practice swinging the bat with his friends.
Turn to page 22!

3. Elmo can ask his coach for help.
Turn to page 24!

Now, let's **DO**! Turn to solution, **1**, **2**, or **3**.

Elmo watched Abby swing at the ball.

She took a deep breath, made sure her hands were in the right place on the bat, and kept her eyes on the ball. She took a big swing and hit the ball!

Now, it was Elmo's turn. He was still nervous, but he talked to himself to help him feel better. "Elmo can do this! Elmo will take a breath. Elmo will make sure his hands are in the right place. Then Elmo will keep Elmo's eyes on the ball."

Elmo felt calmer and was ready to try. Elmo swung the bat and hit the ball off the tee!

"Zoe and Abby, can you show Elmo how to swing the bat?"

"Sure thing, Elmo!" said Abby. "First, grip the bat with both of your hands."

"Excellent!" said Zoe. "Now, take a practice swing. Like this."

"Great job, Elmo! Are you ready to play?"
"Elmo is ready!"

23

"Coach, can you help Elmo?"

"Absolutely! Let's go over to the tee."

Coach showed Elmo how and where to stand.

Elmo swung.

"Keep your eyes on
the ball, Elmo. You can
do this. Try again."

Elmo swung again.

"Try one more time."
Elmo hit it!
"Go, Elmo! Now, run!"

Elmo and his mommy were visiting a new playground.

"Elmo sees children and monsters digging in the sandbox, running through the sprinklers, and climbing on the jungle gym. Everyone is having fun but Elmo."

Even though Elmo was with his mommy, he didn't know anyone and he didn't know how to make friends. Elmo was feeling **SHY**.

 "Psst! Elmo needs your help. Let's **BREATHE** together! Put your hands on your tummy and take three slow, deep breaths in through your nose and out through your mouth."

Let's **THINK** of three ways to help Elmo feel better.

1. Elmo can offer to share a toy.
Turn to page 30!

2. Elmo can share his bubbles with the monsters. Turn to page 32!

3. Elmo can ask his mommy for help and ideas. Turn to page 34!

Now, let's **DO**! Turn to solution, **1**, **2**, or **3**.

"Are you making sand pies?" Elmo asked a little girl. "Elmo loves making sand pies. Chocolate chippie sand pies, strawberry sand pies . . . Elmo uses the watering can to make his pies! Want to use it?"

"Yes, please! I like making pineapple sand pies!" she said. "Would you like to make some with me?"

"Elmo would like that a lot. Here's some pineapple. Hee hee!"

Elmo wanted to run through the sprinklers, but he was too shy to ask.
Maybe if he shares his bubbles, they can all play together.

"Mommy, Elmo is feeling shy. Will you help Elmo make some friends?"

"Sure, Elmo. I see an open swing next to those monsters. Why don't you go swing and talk to them?"

"Thank you, Mommy! Elmo loves to swing and make new friends."

Elmo was sitting with his mommy and daddy on the couch. They reminded him that he had a doctor's appointment after lunch. He was going to be getting a shot.

Elmo didn't know what to expect.

"Maybe Elmo will hide in the closet. That way Elmo won't have to go to the doctor."

Elmo did not like shots. He was feeling **SCARED.**

 "Psst! Elmo needs your help. Let's **BREATHE** together! Put your hands on your tummy and take three slow, deep breaths in through your nose and out through your mouth."

Now, let's **THINK** of three ways to help Elmo feel better.

1. Elmo can talk to his mommy about being scared. Turn to page 40!

2. Elmo can play doctor with Zoe. Turn to page 42!

3. Elmo can bring a favorite toy to his appointment. Turn to page 44!

Now, let's **DO**! Turn to solution, **1**, **2**, or **3**.

"Mommy, why does Elmo have to get a shot?"

"Well, Elmo, it's important to take care of ourselves and stay healthy.

We all have to get shots, even mommies and daddies!"

"Elmo is scared to get a shot," Elmo whispered.

"That's okay, my little Elmo. I get scared sometimes, too. But I will be with you the whole time, I promise."

"Zoe, have you ever had to get a shot?" asked Elmo.

"I just got one last week, Elmo," said Zoe. "It only hurt for a minute, and I got a cool bandage on my arm!"

"Elmo is scared of getting a shot."

"I have an idea, Elmo! Let's pretend you're taking Baby David to get a shot. I'll be the doctor."

"Baby David wants to know what it feels like," said Elmo.

"It feels like a little pinch," said Zoe.

Dr. Zoe cleaned Baby David's arm while Elmo gave him a big hug.

"One, two, three. All done!" said Dr. Zoe. She gave Baby David a pretend shot.

"What's that, Baby David? That wasn't so bad after all!"

"Hi, Elmo! I see you have some friends with you."

"This is my mommy and Baby David. Doctor, does Elmo have to get a shot today?"

"Yes, but I promise it will be very quick." The doctor cleaned Elmo's arm.

"One. Two. Three. Done!"

"That's it?" asked Elmo.

"That's it! And here's a special bandage and a sticker for you."

"That wasn't so scary!" said Elmo.

PARENT AND CAREGIVER RESOURCE GUIDE

Just like Elmo, young children are constantly facing new challenges—trying to share, overcoming disappointment when they don't get what they want, or feeling frustration and jealousy. But unlike older children who have the words to express their emotions, preschoolers and young children do not have the language skills to say, *I'm mad because I don't want to share my new toy*; *I'm jealous that I can't do the same things the big kids can*; or *I'm frustrated because I can't button my coat*. Thus, it's no surprise that young children can be overwhelmed by feelings and have a tantrum. Because they do not have the vocabulary to express their frustrations, they might react in a way that's frustrating to you, too. And this is perfectly normal behavior for this age.

Helping Children Identify and
Label Their Emotions

When children are given the words to express themselves, they can better understand their feelings and the feelings of others. Parents and caregivers should encourage children to talk, draw, or write about their feelings and help them find the words to express, identify, and understand those emotions. For example: *I see you're angry because John grabbed your pail without asking first*; or *Ginger, I can see you're tired. It's hard building a castle when you're tired. Maybe you should do it first thing in the morning after you have a good night's sleep.*

Identifying and labeling feelings can also help children understand and differentiate between the many different emotions they're experiencing. Here are some useful phrases to encourage children to reflect on and better express their emotions:

"We can work together."

"How may I help you?"

"How can we solve that problem?"

"Are we okay now?"

"What are you feeling?"

"I can tell you're feeling . . ."

"Let's talk about it."

"Are you okay?"

"What can I do?"

"What will help you feel better?"

Having the words to describe their feelings helps children reflect rather than react. Children will also be better able to distinguish between the many different feelings they may be experiencing (for example, sad vs. tired, angry vs. jealous, angry vs. tired vs. scared). They will also be more receptive to the feelings of others.

Likewise, children who are attuned to changes in people's body language and facial expressions, as well as the uncomfortable physical feelings in their own bodies when they are frustrated, sad, worried, or angry, can better manage their emotions. This will help them develop stronger, more meaningful friendships and help them as they learn to cooperate and share with others.

BREATHE, THINK, DO
is as easy as learning your A, B, C, D, and E's.

ASK what's the problem? How are they feeling?

BRAINSTORM solutions.

CHOOSE. Find a mutually acceptable solution.

DO! Support and praise your children as they implement a solution.

EVALUATE. How well did the solution work? If it didn't, go back to your brainstormed solutions and keep trying!